HOOPS
— HOORAY! —
CREATIVE IDEAS FOR EMBROIDERY HOOPS & MORE

LEISURE ARTS, INC. • Maumelle, Arkansas

CONTENTS

ABOUT THE AUTHOR

Ashley Millhouse is from Lancaster, Pennsylvania and has been crafting and designing for as long as she can remember. After studying art and earning a BFA in Communication Design, she now works as an Art Director, Designer, and Stylist at a home décor company. Her crafting passions include sewing, weaving, and designing new projects to decorate her home.

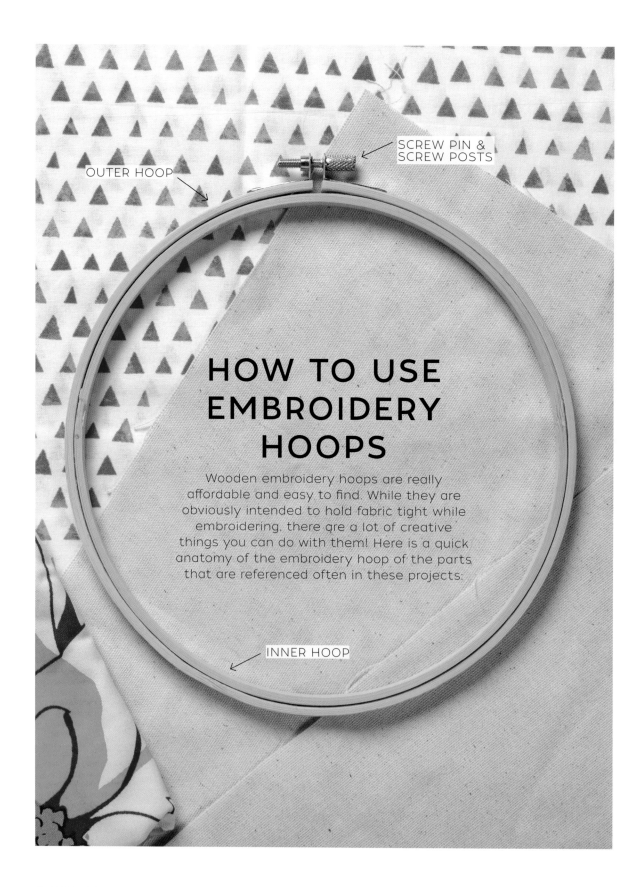

OUTER HOOP

SCREW PIN &
SCREW POSTS

HOW TO USE EMBROIDERY HOOPS

Wooden embroidery hoops are really affordable and easy to find. While they are obviously intended to hold fabric tight while embroidering, there are a lot of creative things you can do with them! Here is a quick anatomy of the embroidery hoop of the parts that are referenced often in these projects:

INNER HOOP

WHAT YOU NEED

Here are some basic tools and materials that you will
need for many of the projects in this book:

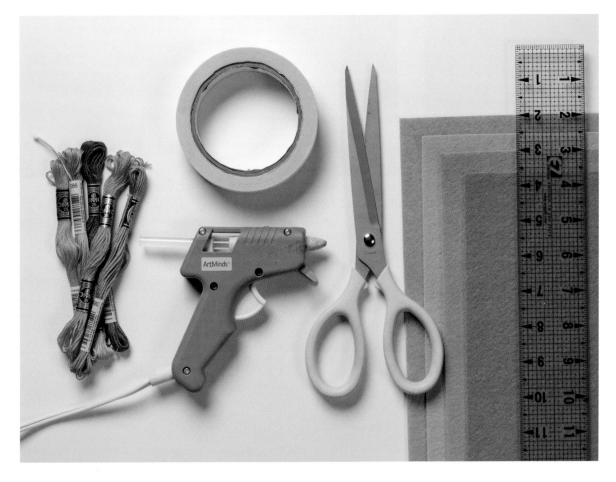

SHARP SCISSORS
You will definitely want
good sharp scissors,
particularly for cutting felt.

HOT GLUE GUN
A hot glue gun is every
crafter's best tool. You can
stick anything to anything!

CLEAR RULER
A clear quilter's ruler is
really helpful to have
on hand.

PAPER-BACKED FUSIBLE
WEB
This a perfect for doing
appliqué work. It is usually
sold in the sewing notions
section of the craft store.

MASKING TAPE
This is always good to
have within reach.

FELT AND FELT POM-POMS
Felt is really versatile and
is used in a variety of ways
throughout the book.

FINISHING OPTIONS

I use two different methods for finishing fabric projects. Each project includes the method I used for that project, but you can use whichever one works best for you.

 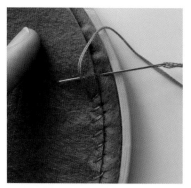 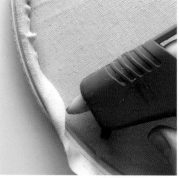

SEWN METHOD: This method is the traditional way to finish embroidery if it is going to be displayed in the hoop. This works best for heavier fabrics, like felt. I also prefer this for projects that have a lot of stitching to hide on the backside. Described in more detail on page 33, Wanderlust Hoop.

HOT GLUE METHOD: Hot glue is a quick and easy way to finish your project. This worked best for cotton fabric or if your project has other embellishments that are secured in the hoop. Described in more detail on page 22, Felt Flower Hoop.

HOOP EMBELLISHMENTS

A variety of embellishments can be added to wooden hoops. Use any of these ideas for any project to add your own twist to the design.

 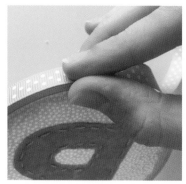 

PAINTING THE HOOP: Use 1 or 2 layers of craft paint that match your design.

ADDING RIBBON: Use a small amount of hot glue to adhere ½" ribbon to the outside of your hoop.

WRAPPING THE HOOP: Add texture to a wreath design by wrapping twine or rope around the inner hoop.

BRASS HOOPS

Gold or brass hoops are intended to be used as a base for macramé, but they can create a modern base for a lot of creative ideas. You can find them with weaving items at your local craft store in a variety of sizes.

DIFFICULTY RATINGS

Each project has a difficulty rating, but all of these projects can be achieved with basic crafting techniques.

SUPER EASY:
Uses basic crafting techniques, minimal materials, and can be done quickly.

VERY EASY:
Uses basic crafting techniques, more variety of materials, and takes more time to complete.

EASY:
Requires slightly more advanced techniques, a wide variety of materials and longer to complete.

MODERN MOBILE

MATERIALS:

- 8" Embroidery hoop
- White embroidery floss
- 30 Felted pom-poms

Add mid-century modern whimsy to your nursery or playroom with a colorful mobile. This project is super fast and easy; you can make this in less than an hour!

STRINGING THE POM-POMS

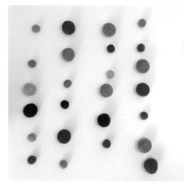

STEP 1: Gather all of your supplies and cut the embroidery floss into five 46" pieces. Line up the pom-poms in 5 rows how you want to string them.

STEP 2: Thread your embroidery needle and tie a small knot at the end to secure the first pom-pom. Continue adding, keeping even spacing (about 3"). Repeat for all 5 strands.

PUTTING IT TOGETHER

STEP 3: Wrap the end of a strand around the inner hoop 2-3 times making sure the that the ends extend about 10" above the hoop. Evenly space 3 more strands around the hoop. Add the outer hoop and close to secure the four strands.

STEP 4: Gather the 4 ends and add the remaining pom-pom strand to the center. Make sure they are all even and tie in a knot. Take all 5 strands and tie into a loop for hanging. Use a small cup hook to hang from the ceiling.

EVERYDAY WREATH

MATERIALS:

- 12" Inner embroidery hoop
- Hot glue
- Twine
- Faux peony, greens and berry branches

A large embroidery hoop provides a perfect blank canvas for this floral wreath. Wrapping the inner hoop in twine gives this project rustic farmhouse charm.

WRAPPING THE HOOP

STEP 1: Wrap the inner hoop with twine, covering hoop completely. Secure the beginning and end of the section by wrapping over it. Glue the final end with hot glue.

ARRANGING THE FLORALS

STEP 2: Cut apart the florals, removing the stem from the peony and cutting a few individual leaves off the stem.

STEP 3: Arrange and glue the florals, starting with the leaf stem and then the berry branches. Glue the peony in the center.

STEP 4: Layer a few single leaves around the peony.

MINIMAL BRASS WREATH

MATERIALS:

- 12" Brass hoop
- Hot glue
- Wire cutters
- Faux boxwood
- Faux ranaculous in a variety of sizes
- Faux lamb's ear leaves
- 2.5" wide striped ribbon, approximately 16"

The brass hoop makes this simple design very modern and stylish. The boxwoods are seasonless, so you can hang this on your door during any season.

BEFORE YOU GET STARTED

Try making felt flowers instead of fake ones. The daisy or carnation on page 20 would work perfectly with this design.

ARRANGING THE FLORALS

STEP 1: Arrange the boxwood and leaves symmetrically on the brass hoop. To glue, hold the boxwood to the hoop and flip over. Apply hot glue in between the hoop and greens and hold in place until glue dries.

STEP 3: Flip the hoop to front and glue leaves in place over the boxwood.

STEP 4: Apply hot glue to back of flowers and press into place, holding until the glue dries.

STEP 4: Fold the ribbon half and glue on the back of the flowers in a "V" position.

DOILY DREAM CATCHER

MATERIALS:

- 14" Doily
- 12" Embroidery hoop
- Hot glue
- A variety of ribbons and yarn cut into 36" lengths. (For this design, I used 16 strands).

This is a really easy project that looks stunning with both modern and bohemian home décor. You can find doilies like this at your local craft store or thrift shop.

BEFORE YOU GET STARTED

If you want to use a thicker material for the fringes, such as roving yarn, you may need a plastic weaving needle to pull the thick strand through the doily.

SECURING THE DOILY

STEP 1: Evenly drape the doily over the inner hoop. Add the outer hoop, making sure all of the edges are sandwiched between the inner and outer hoop.

STEP 2: Use a few inches of string to tighten the outer hoop. (Due to the thickness of the doily, you won't be able to use the screw pin to tighten the hoop). Tie the string tightly. Don't worry how it looks; we will address this at the end.

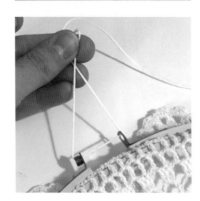

STEP 3: Tighten and center the doily evenly by pulling the edges from the back. Once all the edges are even, flip over and use a thin line of hot glue all the way around to secure.

STEP 4: Once the glue is dry, trim off the excess doily. Touch up any spots you may have missed with the glue.

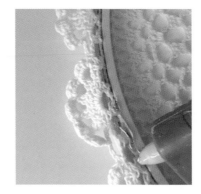

ADDING FRINGE

STEP 5: To add fringe, fold your ribbon or yarn in half and put the two ends through the doily as close to the bottom as you can. Pull the two ends through the loop you made in the front. Pull to tighten. Keep adding fringes until you are satisfied with the fullness.

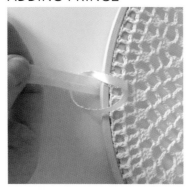

FINISHING

STEP 6: Hold up your dream catcher and trim any fringes that may seem out of place. To finish, remove the string used to tighten the outer hoop and replace with ribbon tied in a bow to give a finished look.

MAKE A MINI!

MINI MATERIALS:

- 4" hoop
- 6" square lace
- Twine or yarn
- Three beads

MINI INSTRUCTIONS:
Follow the same steps for the larger hoop using the lace instead of a doily. Add a bead to the ends of a few strings.

FELT FLOWER HOOP

MATERIALS:

- 10" embroidery hoop
- Hot glue
- Fabric for base
- Variety of felt
- Wool felt pom-poms
- Embroidery needle and floss

Felt flowers are a lot of fun to make and look amazing when bunched together in big groups. The unbleached linen background lets them really shine. You can customize the stitched sentiment with whatever you like-a greeting, a name, or you can leave it blank and add more flowers.

STEP 1: When shopping for your felt, consider your color palette. For the flowers, you will want at least 3 colors that compliment each other. For the leaves, choose 2 shades of green to add depth.

CHOOSING YOUR COLORS

Copy the pattern needed by photocopying or tracing onto plain paper. Use the pattern as a guide to cut out your felt pieces. If you want to trace the pattern directly onto the felt, make sure to use a pencil and not a marker or pen. Ink lines will bleed into the felt and be very hard to remove.

MAKING THE FLOWERS: DAISY

STEP 1: Cut four daisies out of felt (see pattern on page 48).

STEP 2: Fold in half once and glue; fold in half again and glue. Repeat for all.

STEP 3: Cut a small square of felt and glue the 4 petals onto it, with all corners meeting in the middle.

STEP 4: Glue a yellow felt pom-pom in the center.

MAKING THE FLOWERS: CARNATION

STEP 1: Cut a 2" x 9" strip of felt. Fold in half and glue. Cut fringes along the folded over edge.

STEP 2: Roll the strip up, keeping the center tight. Glue the end to secure.

You can make these flowers in a variety of sizes, just cut a longer or shorter strip of felt. I added 2 small flowers to my hoop that used a 5" strip of fringes.

MAKING THE FLOWERS: DAHLIAS

STEP 1: Cut 40 dahlia petals (see pattern on page 48). Cut a 5" x 1¼" strip and cut rounded points as shown.

STEP 2: Apply a small amount of glue to the wide end of the petal and pinch. Repeat for all.

STEP 3: Roll the strip of points around itself, keeping the center tight.

STEP 4: Glue the petals to the center, keeping spacing even. The first layer will use 5 petals. Continue adding layers until the flower is full and even.

MAKING THE LEAVES

STEP 1: Cut two large leaves (use the teardrop pattern on page 48 as a guide, make the shape as large or small as you like) from the same green felt. Cut three smaller ones from the second green felt.

EMBROIDERING THE HOOP

STEP 1: Draw the lettering you want to use on paper. For a 10" hoop, the lettering should be about 7" long. Trace over the pencil with a black marker.

STEP 2: Transfer the letter to your fabric by taping the paper to a sunny window. Tape your fabric on top and lightly trace with a pencil.

STEP 3: Center your traced lettering in your hoop. Running stitch the lettering, keeping tight spacing between each stitch.

STEP 4: Cut the fabric around the hoop to ½" and glue to the inside.

ADDING THE FLOWERS

STEP 5: Arrange your flowers and leaves on the hoop. Remove just the flowers and glue the leaves down. Glue the largest flowers first then the smallest Add a few pom-poms to fill in an empty spots.

Want to make felt succulents instead of flowers? Make the dahlias in different shades of greens, blues and even reds. Use different amounts of petals to vary the size of your succulents. The larger ones use 20 petals, the small one uses 5.

● ● ● ● GIFT TAGS

I love adding a little handmade flair to gifts. These gift tags made using small embroidery hoops are easy to pull together and add the perfect touch to any gift, or can even be the gift themselves!

GIFT TAGS:
MONOGRAM TAG

MATERIALS:

- 4" Embroidery hoop
- Hot glue
- 8" x 8" fabric
- 2½" letter pattern
- Embroidery floss
- Embroidery needle
- ½" Ribbon
- Paper-backed fusible web

APPLYING THE LETTER

STEP 1: Adhere the fusible web to the felt and draw your letter pattern.. Make sure the letter is **BACKWARDS** at this step. Cut out and remove paper backing.

STEP 2: Adhere the letter onto the fabric and center in the hoop. Stitch around the edges with floss.

FINISHING

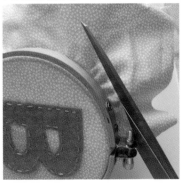

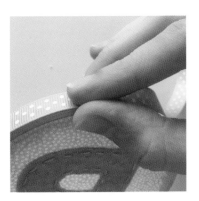

STEP 3: Trim the fabric to ½" and hot glue to the inside of the hoop.

STEP 4: Apply a small amount of hot glue to the outside of the hoop and press the ribbon into it, aligning with the edges. Tie a bow around the screw to hang.

GIFT TAGS:
LOVE NOTE

MATERIALS:

- 4" Embroidery hoop
- Hot glue
- Red paint
- 8" x 8" fabric
- 3" x 3" felt heart
- Embroidery floss
- Coordinating ribbon
- Foam paintbrush

PREPARING THE HOOP

STEP 1: Paint the outer hoop. You may need to apply two coats to get a bright color. Let dry completely.

STEP 2: Put the fabric in hoop, pull tight and secure the pin.

MAKING THE HEART POCKET

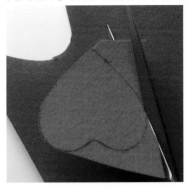

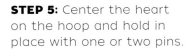

STEP 3: Trace and cut out the pattern on page 48. Trace pattern onto the felt and cut out.

STEP 4: Running stitch along the top half of the heart. Keep the needle and thread attached when you reach the end.

STEP 5: Center the heart on the hoop and hold in place with one or two pins.

STEP 6: Resume stitching around the heart, sewing through the fabric. Work all the way around, tying off the thread when finished.

FINISHING

STEP 7: Trim the fabric to about ½". Apply hot glue to the inside of the hoop and adhere the fabric.

STEP 8: Tie a coordinating ribbon hanger and bow around the hoop screw. In the pocket, you can hide a little love note or keepsake.

BIRTHDAY GIFT CARD HOLDER

MATERIALS:

- 4" Embroidery hoop
- Hot glue
- 8" x 8" fabric and a piece of 8" x 6" fabric
- Embroidery floss
- 2-3 small fabric scraps
- Paper-backed fusible web
- Coordinating ribbon
- Embroidery needle

MAKING THE PENNANT

STEP 1: Fold over the long edge of the 8" x 6" fabric ½" and press to make the pocket.

STEP 2: Adhere the fusible web to the fabric. Trace the pennant pattern onto plain paper. Use the pattern to cut out 1-2 pieces from each fabric.

STEP 3: Peel off the backing from the pennants and arrange on the pocket, using the inner hoop as a guide for placement Fuse in place.

STITCHING THE ROPE

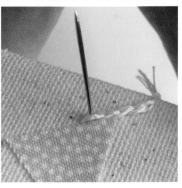

STEP 4: Using embroidery floss, stitch across the pennants using a split stitch. To split stitch, make one straight stitch. Bring your needle back up through the middle of your previous stitch. Repeat along the entire length of the triangles.

FINISHING

STEP 5: Layer the finished pocket fabric over the back fabric, leaving 1½" from the top of the hoop to the top of the pocket. Place the top hoop over all layers and tighten.

STEP 6: Trim the fabric edge to about ½". Use hot glue to secure to the inside of the hoop. Finish by adding a coordinating ribbon bow and hanger to hang or attach to a gift.

WANDERLUST HOOP

Inspired by vintage camping patches, this design is easy to customize with your favorite colors. Check out the mini version at the end to see how small design elements can totally change the look.

BEFORE YOU GET STARTED

You can do appliqué without the paper-backed fusible web, but it is really helpful to use. You can draw your patterns clearly on the paper backing before adhering the fusible web to the felt, and when you remove the backing your piece is like an iron-on sticker.

STEP 1: Trace the inner edge of the inner hoop to your backing felt. Cut out and set aside for later.

STEP 2: Adhere the fusible web to the appliqué felt. Copy or trace the pattern pieces on page 48 onto plain paper. Draw around the pattern on the paper backing on the felt. Cut out the appliqués. Peel off the paper backing.

PREPPING MATERIALS

STEP 3: Arrange your appliqué pieces on the main felt inside the outer hoop. When you are happy with the arrangement, remove the hoop and adhere the design with your iron. Make sure the edges of the pieces are well secured. Center the design inside the hoop and secure.

APPLIQUÉ

STEP 4: Using a running stitch, sew around the edge of each piece with coordinating floss. Continue for all appliqué pieces.

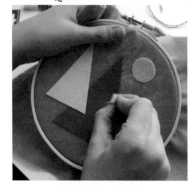

FINISHING

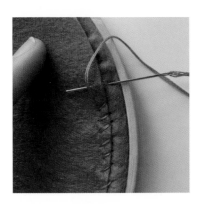

STEP 5: Trim the outer edge of the felt, leaving at least 1" all around.

STEP 6: Sew a long basting stitching around the felt, staying close to the edge. Pull the ends tight, bringing all of the felt inside the hoop. Knot the ends.

STEP 7: Place the backing felt on top of the gathered felt and whip stitch through the gathered felt and backing felt all the way around the edge.

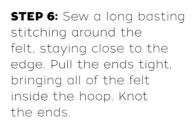

MAKE A MINI!

MINI MATERIALS:

- 4" hoop
- White felt
- White embroidery floss
- Black polka dot fabric

MINI INSTRUCTIONS:

Follow the same steps for the larger hoop using two small triangles and a crescent moon shape. Arrange in the 4" hoop and add a few "X" stitches for stars.

CRAFT ORGANIZATION

Using embroidery hoops to decorate and organize your craft space is a no brainer. These projects are functional and super cute!

SIMPLE POCKET

MATERIALS:

- 8" Embroidery hoop
- 12" x 12" Background fabric
- 12" x 8" Pocket fabric
- 8" x 8" Felt for backing
- Embroidery floss

Making this pocket is easy and quick. You can make one in any size to store pens, scissors, glasses, anything you need to keep close by while you work.

MAKING THE POCKET

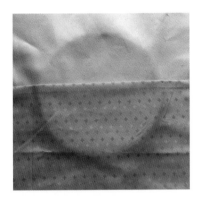

STEP 1: Trace the inner edge of the inner hoop to your backing felt. Cut out and set aside for later.

STEP 2: Fold over the long edge of your pocket fabric ½" and press. Fold over again and press.

STEP 3: Place background fabric over the inner hoop and then layer your pocket fabric on top, about 3" from the top. Place outer hoop over inner and tighten.

FINISHING

STEP 4: Trim the fabric to about 1" all around.

STEP 5: Sew a basting stitch around the edge of the trimmed fabric. Pull tight and tie the ends together.

STEP 6: Place the felt backing over the gathered edge and whip stitch around the entire edge.

CRAFT ORGANIZATION:
PIN CUSHION

MATERIALS:

- 4" Embroidery hoop
- 8" x 8" fabric
- Fiberfill
- Hot glue
- 4" x 4" cardboard
- 4" x 4" felt for backing

A pin cushion is an essential crafting item. The flat backing on this design lets it hang on the wall or sit flat on your desk.

CREATING THE BASE

STEP 1: Trace the inside edge of the inner hoop onto the cardboard and the felt. Cut out both and set felt aside.

STEP 2: Glue the cardboard circle into the inner hoop. Let glue dry completely.

STUFFING THE CUSHION

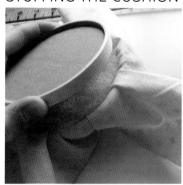

STEP 3: Pull your fabric through the front of the outer hoop and stuff with fiberfill. Place the back into the hoop. Make sure fabric and fiberfill are even before tightening the hoop.

FINISHING

STEP 4: Trim the excess fabric, leaving about 1" all around. Glue the fabric to the cardboard back. To finish, glue the felt circle onto the back, covering the cardboard and fabric edges completely.

CRAFT ORGANIZATION:
CLIP BOARD HOOP

MATERIALS:

- 14" Embroidery hoop
- Hot Glue
- 20" x 20" main fabric
- 20" x 20" white backing fabric (optional)
- Small wooden clothespins
- Twine

Finish off your craft organizing with this fun clip board. Keep notes and pattern pieces in close reach or to decorate with photos.

Depending on the weight of your main fabric, you may want to add a second fabric for stability. I used quilting cotton for my main fabric and added a layer of white muslin for the backing.

LAYERING THE FABRIC AND TWINE

STEP 1: Layer the fabric and twine over the inner hoop. Arrange the twine in zigzag pattern (highlighted in blue).

STEP 2: Place the outer hoop over all layers and tighten about halfway. Work all the way around, pulling the fabric and twine tight Tighten completely

FINISHING

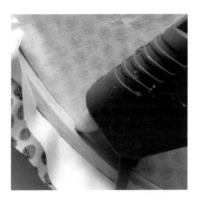

STEP 3: Trim the fabric to ½" all around, leaving twine long. Apply a small amount of hot glue to the inside of the hoop and press the fabric into it. If you used two layers of fabric, you will need to do this twice, gluing the first layer to the hoop and the second to the first fabric.

STEP 4: Trim the twine ends to about 1" and glue to the inside rim of the hoop.

STEP 5: Flip to front and add about 5 mini clothespins to the twine.

BOHO RIBBON CHANDELIER

MATERIALS:

- 12" Inner embroidery hoop
- 4½' string of battery operated LED lights
- Variety of ribbons and lace, about 30 yards total
- Masking tape
- Twine

Fringe chandeliers are really fun for party decor, or for any time! You use any combination of colors, or use white yarn for a 70's vibe.

BEFORE YOU GET STARTED

When you go shopping for materials, make sure to get twinkle lights with a small battery pack. A larger one that requires 2-3 batteries will be too heavy for the chandelier.

You can use any variety of ribbons for this project, but keep the width 1½" or less. The more variation of materials, the more interesting the final project will be!

STEP 1: Cut your ribbon and lace into 36" lengths and arrange into like color groups on your desktop.

STEP 2: Cut four pieces of twine each 36" long. Fold in half and knot around the inner hoop, spaced evenly. Tie the ends together in a loose knot. These will eventually be used to hang the finished chandelier.

PREPPING MATERIALS

ATTACHING THE RIBBON

STEP 3: Add the ribbon starting with the color you have the most of and working towards the one you have the least of. I started with white and grey, and the last ribbons I added only have one or two pieces.

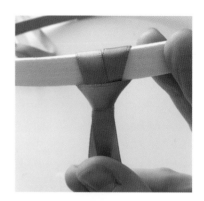

STEP 4: Fold the ribbon in half and hold the loop on the front of the hoop. Pull the ends through the loop and pull down. Repeat for all ribbons, distributing each color evenly.

STEP 5: Gather up the four twine strands. Adjust the twine until the hoop hangs straight. Tie all of the twine ends together.

ADDING THE TWINKLE LIGHTS

STEP 6: Hide the battery pack behind a large piece of ribbon. Secure it to the hoop with a 1" piece of masking tape (tape works best in case you need to remove the pack to replace the batteries).

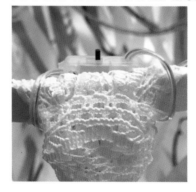

STEP 7: Wrap the light wire around the hoop, keeping the spacing between the lights even.

Embroidery hoops are a great way to show off beautiful fabrics. Use 5 or more hoops in a variety of sizes to create a gallery wall of all your favorite prints.

DIP-DYED FIBER HANGING

MATERIALS:

- 10" Brass hoop
- 12" Brass hoop
- Hot glue
- 16 yards of 100% cotton yarn/cord
- One 4" faux succulent + 2 other smaller varieties
- Powdered fabric dye
- Plastic drop cloth
- Stainless steel bowl
- Masking tape

Fiber wall decor is super popular right now. This project incorporates a lot of simple techniques that come together to create a really interesting piece of home décor.

BEFORE YOU GET STARTED

You will want to use 100% cotton for the dip-dyed fringes. Nylon or polyester blends do not absorb the dye as evenly, so pay close attention to the fiber content when you are shopping for supplies.

STEP 1: Cut the cord into 36" lengths. Set aside one for the hanger. To attach them to the 12" hoop, fold a cord in half placing the loop on the front of the hoop. Pull the ends through the loop and pull tight. Continue for all 15 strands.

ADDING THE FRINGE

TRIM THE FRINGE

STEP 2: Lay the hoop and fringe flat on your surface. Make sure none of the strands are overlapping. Using masking tape, create a point. Cut along the edge of the tape. Remove and discard the tape.

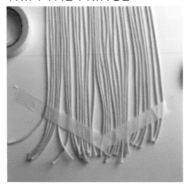

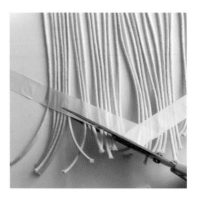

DIP DYING

STEP 3: Cover your work space with a plastic drop cloth. Fill a stainless steel bowl with water and presoak about 10" of the fringe. Let it soak for about 15 minutes.

STEP 4: Add a few spoonfuls of powdered dye to your water. Stir to dissolve. Do a few tests to check the color.

STEP 5: Dip about 6" of the presoaked fringe into the dye. The dye will creep up the wet cord creating an ombre effect. Leave in the dye for about 15 minutes or until you are happy with the color. The longer you let it soak the darker the color will get. Hang your piece over the drop cloth to dry completely; overnight is best.

ATTACHING SECOND HOOP

STEP 6: Center the 10" hoop and align it to the top. For the hanger, add the remaining cord using the same method as the fringes.

GLUING THE SUCCULENTS

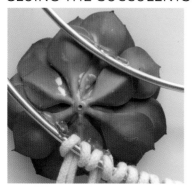 

STEP 7: Start by adding the large succulent. It should be larger enough to touch both brass hoops. Add a small dab of hot glue at each spot that the succulent touches the brass hoops. Allow glue to dry completely. Flip over and apply more glue to ensure the succulent is fully attached. Let hot glue dry completely before flipping back over.

STEP 8: Arrange and glue on the remaining succulents.

PATTERNS

Love Note

Felt Flower Hoop

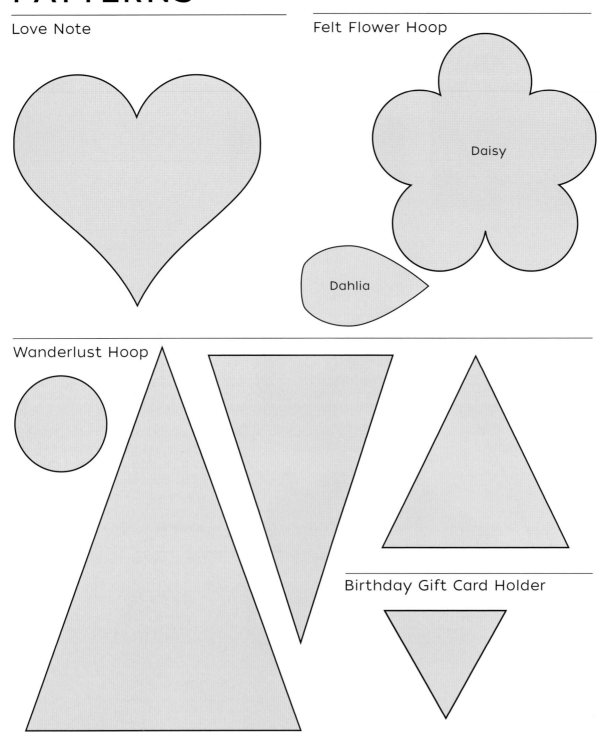

Daisy

Dahlia

Wanderlust Hoop

Birthday Gift Card Holder

Made in the U.S.A.

We have made every effort to ensure that these instructions are accurate and complete. We cannot, however, be responsible for human error, typographical mistakes, or variations in individual work.